Reverence

Poornima Dayal

BookLeaf
Publishing

India | USA | UK

Made with ❤ on the BookLeaf Publishing Platform
www.bookleafpub.in
www.bookleafpub.com

Dedication

I dedicate this book to all those moments of my life that
have inspired me to write this book.
I am grateful to The Divine.

Preface

Hi friends,

This book is about the expression of Reverence. It is about living in Gratitude.

I am an artist, more precisely a painter by profession. I paint on Canvas and my companionship with art is over three decades old.

In this book, I have tried to put my journey as an artist in the form of poetry.

I believe in living in reverence to The Divine and this book of poems goes on to explain how that has helped me with my art and daily living.

This book narrates poems from my real life experiences, some fictional dreams and few of them also go on to illustrate the artworks I do.

This book is about getting transparent, about baring it all which is also represented by one of my poem's in this book titled, ' Transparency' .

Hope you enjoy reading my poems.

In eternal Gratitude.

Poornima Dayal.

note - The he, him, his , Thou, Thee, Ye (poetic references) in this book may refer to God

Acknowledgements

I am extremely grateful to the divine for bringing me this opportunity to express my gratitude to the Almighty.
I am thankful to my son, my husband, my mother and my pet for propelling me forward.
Thank you.
I would also like to thank the readers for taking out time to read these poems.
Let me know which poem really caught your fancy.

Best.

Poornima Dayal.

1. Creator

One is he, my creator.
In unison are his ways and creations.
My beloved God, not veiled
but living in us all - in all.
Through the charming night
and the day, where there is light.
Across rivers and seas,
lofty hills and frosty peaks.
In sand and Earth
so there ain't no dearth.

Wearing his kingly, Silken robes
of illuminating light
our revered, holy, real knight.
Benevolent, compassionate, kind is he
tolerant, affable and tender.

Hearing our pleas
day in and out
even when humans scream or shout.

Quiet is he, yet all ears
precious are his ways,
bringing all cheer.
Oh my dear, be not so far
for he is near
and always the first one to hear.

Free me, hug me, set me up
to be Thy child up and close.
So I may rant and scribble heartily all my woes.

Teach me gratitude the plain-sailing way
and how to intently love every June and May.

2. Reverence

REVERENCE

From the depths of my heart,
from within the joys of living,
there's a whisper, albeit sometimes a roar,
ready to be heard
told aloud
spoken and expressed.

Tears of unspoken words and joy
come pouring down
sometimes on canvas or on paper.
Reds, Blues, Crimson and Prestine Whites,
as new chapters unfold
one story leading to another,
I bow in gratitude
for what may have been, for what is and for what will
be.

Remaining untarnished, nourished
in the rays of Thy love,
I surrender and bow
as the artist in me unfurls,
yet another tale of contentment,
joy, learning and gratitude.

3. Love at first sight

I saw you, You saw me.
it was love at first sight.
I knew it somewhere, somehow
we were at the same place for a reason.
When sparks glittered , I knew it to be a Divine sign.
Those Purples, Bold Ochre, Olives
were calling out to be splashed and splattered.
I knew he was guiding me
to love and express,
to care and caress.

I am all a part of You,
humbled forever by your sublime presence.
beatitude, gratitude.

Look , He holds my hands
as the brush strikes it's strokes,
as colours fill the palette magically.
As hardy tools meneuver their ways
through the grains of the brand new canvas.

I see - I see an enchanting wave,
oh, a line just found it's habitat
leaving me ever enamored of The supreme, Divine ways.

Did you notice the cityscape,
an artists saga or a poetic fairy tale.
Lo and behold, such diverse expressions and creations
how magnificent and magnanimous is his glorious
radiation
unending, eternal, superfluous and infinite.

4. Transparency

Dabbling in Whites and rustic Reds
with Emerald Green and Turquoise Blues
lining, edging its passive borders.

Over are days and nights so tough
over is that land of shifts.
Agony, pain are but now of the past
in God's Divine name are the White and Red cast.

With open landscapes
and lots to explore,
within new cityscapes
there's so much more
to live, breathe and enjoy.

In reverence, I bow
no limits to thankfulness.
An open book with fresh, leafy pages
speaking of love, few sadhus and sages.
Nothing to hide

no more to disclose
just that art where it's all right and composed.
New messages from the stars, The Sun, The Moon arise
painted in this new series that's all about Sunrise.

5. Birth

The box opened to a new beginning
with Acrylics reigning and storytelling.
Thanking his grace, began this journey
in the subtle warmth of Spring.

Those shinning Pansies, Cherry Bougainvilleas
and lush Green trees,
dancing to swift winds.
The murmuring Myna's
drinking sips of of water
from the shores of my verandah.
My canvas set on its gigantic , Teak wood easel
inviting the excited artist in me.

Blues, oh my God ,the way you drive me,
must be love.
Must be a soulmate connection.
Laughing, enjoying your company
I begin a new art piece,
its early 2020.

The days are getting longer
the Sun shone bright
streaming through the windows
reflecting on the almost empty board.
Uncorking the radiant, Navy,
dabbing my brush in water, I begin
with reverence, with a half baked image of what may be.

I draw 'Morrocco', colouring it Red and bright Yellow.
unburdening the heart, baring emotions,
unfurling a jist of what may have been.

Past- past- past, its over.
Hallelujah.

6. Inspiration

Californian Poppies are blossoming,
promising to be true.
It's early Summer, an Orange hue.
The Sun shone bright,
a clear clue
to the brightest future
bringing forth the right suitor.

Offering these flowers do I proceed
to paths of glory where I may succeed.
Their Earthy smell
and saffron twists
their lengthy garlands
having filled my fists.

Hopeful as I am of a happy, new day
of many good beginnings coming my way,
making an obeisance
I incline,
trusting his might, truly divine.

Californian Poppies are beaming
cascading in shrines and
around many a chimes
telling me just so many times
of his continual existence,
of his presence even in this rhyme.

7. Pet Love

I love you baby
love you so.
Just so much more than words could show.
Your gritty teeth
and eyes so sure
oh my baby, I love you so.
For God has made you special,
for me, for us - a family of four.
Thank he, for his mercies are vast
his creation are you,
so cute and ever to last.
My prayer for you, a humble one
is to keep you well and safe.
May the Lord be praised
as you are so much fun to raise.

That tuft of curly hair on your bushy tail
as it swishes - swashes along
grateful am I for this universe where we belong.

Did you just wink, ha, or so I think
chewing that toy, the wrapper apart.
A Cream, popping doggy toy
with circular rings, relishing plastic Chips Ahoy.

' Good morning baby ', and I say my fond hello
upon hearing your voice right now so mellow.
My Goldilocks, with beaming locks
and those eyes so true,
wearing Blue.
When tiptoeing in the mornings you come
narrating woes of the night before.

' Scratchy - wratchy doo ', as I refer
lovingly to your impish ways
telling you much as I fondly gaze.
My child, my puppy now a lady
marvelling at you am I daily.
Come to me, oh little one
may we play with brushes and pen,
with furry cats and big, fat hen.

8. Childhood memories

Dorris and Rosy
my friends and caretakers
when my parents are away.
My playmate Dorris
this dusky, young lady
with chubby, rounded cheeks
baking sweet meats and moist Plum cakes,
every Christmas she brings
a basket of goodies
and crispy breads.

Her older sister, Rosy
very feminine and polite,
taking me in her loving lap
singing a hymn or two,
patting me adoringly.
She and her gorgeous mom Charollete,
regaling me with stories from the Bible,
about Baby Jesus and his birth,
about the Holy Apostles.

Lucky am I to be ever immersed
in the glory of such divinity,
at my parents home,
in their prayer room.

Soaked in such love and cuddles
I learn to appreciate,
to know about the supremacy of sacred shrines.

Growing up could never be more fun,
picking Purple Daisies along my way.
Swarn Singh, our house help since dad's teenage
taking my stroller along the picturesque park.
Ah, everyday is a glorious painting
illustrated by Mother Nature.
Perhaps, getting my sense of colours from there,
gaining experiences from this joyful life.

I write today with paints and brush
effusive notes on my precious canvas.

....Immersed in such love and cuddles
I learn to appriciate.

9. This was another day

This was another day,
I didn't want to be bottled up.
Had enough of holding back
and not letting go.

Maroon said the bottle,
shaking and quivering
every last ounce of it
drizzling on paper.
Permanent Green, Black and Rust
began to scribble a tale of two cities.

So now I know
where this love comes from
of sketching cityscapes and
colossal landscapes
may be leading me to unravel
certain dramas of life,
till then undisclosed.

Croatia, here I come
did you see two painted, abstract figures,
a child hidden in the midst of Olive bushes,
a pet playing in mini Corn fields.

Embracing myself, I congratulate
and thank the artist above.
His ideas, his marvels
his kindness and compassion
is like a pure treasure trove.

Day breaks into a sultry evening
but slipping into a sparkling night.
I hear crackers, yes, Fire crackers
flashing, zapping, zooming outside my window.

(note -this poem talks about my two artworks -
Morocco and Croatia).

10. Garden of love

Living a life of what I feel is required
of me now.
It makes me happy
helping me recognise
my connection.

I love myself and its easy
There's no guilt, no fear.
Just the desire for
more and more gratitude.

What I see before me is
the 'Garden of love'.
A painting with Daisy Pink and Mustard Yellow.
A rising hillock, a vast, deep sky.
Black lines gilding across the Yellows.
That inspiring, delicate ray of good hope
running across its expansive breadth.

Yes, from somewhere within the

confines of my fantasies
did arise this fountain
of visualisation,
experimenting with my mixed emotions,
a melange of artistic styles
and moods galore.

Lending it finishing touches,
I rever, offering surprise at such variants
never knowing the depths of what may lie within
unwrapping such valuable mysteries.

11. Love

A touch with fondness,
a touch of Prayer
a touch filled with love
leaves an undeniable impression in the heart.
It touched a chord.
Left a note to recollect,
to affectionately recall.

The day we met, I knew He held me
your gentle touch, your subtle hints.
Leaving me enchanted and mesmerised.
What a start. I was enthralled, bedazzled
by such gestures of affection.

Did I know you in my past life
or did you ever meet me when I was younger
just doesn't matter
the where and when of it all.

Giving me a go, he signalled from above

soothing my heart tenderly.
Give it a try, he reassured, its all good
in my hands it is and will always be.

How do I thank Thee
for words I don't have
enough to even offer Ye
my gratefulness.

Is it possible through my art
or may be hidden in the
profundity of these poems
is just a wee bit of thankfulness
I may extend towards you.

Thanks for taking me to people who
assured and restored my faith in you.
Who helped me see a path ahead
every now and then providing me the
much needed comfort
to joyfully propel through few tricky tracks.

Life is a road much travelled, make it easy
keep it simple and jolly.
Cheering yourself, helping yourself
staying out of the so called bumpyy terrains.

12. My puppets wedding

It wIas celebration time
my amazing puppet to marry her boy muppet.
A floral marriage hall was fashioned,
with Lillies and Virginia Grapevines
with fragrant, best Dahlia flowers.
Those Red satin ribbons
wavy and dancing in the winds,
tall Ashoka trees, protecting the lofty boundaries.

It was a tea party,
with dear friends and cousins,
a ceremonious cake cutting
and lots of Blue berry muffins.

Did she look pretty,
in her Scarlet wedding dress
head covered with Gold and stunning starlets.
My charming, petite girl
was to marry her
ever so attractive

prince of hearts.

Entered the groom,
our house lit
with shimmering lights
and Halogen bulbs.

As their eyes met, a radiant love transpired
so heavenly, so mighty and noble.
Similar to God's elevated presence,
equivalent to his exalted Godliness.

When two hearts combine
this is what his love is about
unity, integrity and oneness.

Creating such fantasies,
creating the unforgettable
such joy, such unions, such ecstasy.

Revere - Revere - Revere.
Never ending tales of captivating romance
entwining, interweaving, serenading
to his harmonious melodies.

13. His wonders

Its not an illusion - this life.
In reality was it created.
When God's decided to make this Gigantic Earth,
the enormous waters
and the serene skies above.
Reflecting his grace,
his utmost resplendence.

Luscious trees and plants
heavy bushes and sharp Green grass
delectable fruits and berries,
vegetables - some succulent,
others, hoarse and crisp.
Man and animals
fascinatingly alike
crawling, climbing
swimming, walking
or running.

Such wonders, such fables

such interesting stories we hear and read
of his loving, undeniable force.

No line of demarcation is seen.
Above and below gleams his fame.
Within, outside, around us God lives
we do but exist
in his remarkable heart and soul.

To such an awe inspiring creator, do I salute
and surrender with absolute regard and respect.
Wonder at Thy never exhaustive wonders
just how celestial and beatific.
If only I could see you
or perhaps I do
in every speck of Earth and Ether
of the oceans and seas.

In man, woman and child.

14. The concert

Watching and hearing an endearing concert.
Did it lead me to paths then unknown
of love, fame, pleasure and exultation.

Caring for self,
dancing to drums
moving briskly
to the Electric guitar.
What a super guitarist,
strumming as though there were no end
his fingers warmly seducing
his Purple guitar.

The singer,
a White, American man
about 60 odd years old
with his voice of Gold.
A handsome face with high cheek bones,
a slim, sturdy body,
wearing high -heeled Black shoes.

Under those heavy, fog lights
his Royal Blue shirt,
lacy, glossy and ever appealing.
With hair straight and well combed
a Pruny, Blackish - Brown.

'Everything I do....' as he hums
the crowds cheering thunderously.
Plenty clapping hands,
and others shaking and rejoicing.
Grooving to his mellifluous voice
admiring his daring gut and nerves.
Loud can it be heard
till a distance - till a distance!

As I sway along those beats
little knowing what I ever did
to deserve such fantabulous treats.

Wooing, winning so many hearts
with lover's holding hands
or waltzing with stupendous zing.
Several arms around their women's waists
do many men whirl and twirl around.

Considering myself the chosen one
for night another could not have been.

Oh, such symphony, u earn my heart.
This awesome, splendid
supreme bliss.

15. Makarsankranti festival (an Indian festival)

This little kid I saw, about 8 or 9 years old.
Wearing a cotton, Blue shirt and Black and White
knickers.
In his dainty hands
holding sturdy ropes of a kite,
a charming mix of Orange and Gold.

It was 'Makarsankranti'
a festive occasion.
Million such kites criss crossing
in the cold, wintery skies.

Peering at his kite,
flying across the pavement
with horns blaring somewhere in the oblivion.
This boy, know not I his name
hopped and jumped
in sweet, innocent childlike ways.
And then I see another one,

approaching his pretty Orange one
racing, pacing, tracing up too close.

I am but a passer by
in between this game of chance and luck.
Let not another break its thread
or rebelliously tear his kite apart.

Looking up in sheer joy,
breaking away from any major risk.
Deft are his finger movements
his eyes focussed on victory.
Care not he of another soul
frolicking, scampering, playing around.

Aromas of freshly roasted Sesame balls
and strings of salty savouries, I smell,
this special Sunday afternoon.
Balls of Jaggery and flavourful peanuts,
Coconut dumplings and fried Gram flour rings.
Indian festivals, I say
such unbelievably feasting days.

Bustling fields with long, ripe corn
stalks of Wheat and sweet Sugarcane.

Offering Prayers to his exalted ways
revering, thanking yet again and again.

32

16. The mighty warriors

About the mighty warriors
from my out of box series, I sing.
In Ochre Yellow, Pine Green with tinges of Black,
White and Cadmium Red.
Abstract, dramatic with streaks of Olive.

My spatula gushing across the board
fiery applications, smacking bold strokes.
Drawing elliptical orbits,
an army of ferocious warriors
reflecting a Chinese civil war.

'Am I roaring', I wondered
or letting out a war cry.
A suppressed voice
an anguished emotion dismissing
now erupting through this piece of art.
Lying dormant, not yet extinct,
speaking and innovatively narrating.

'Ching' and 'Chang' two mighty warriors
galloping across the drawing pad.
Raising their shiny, Silvery swords
defending China, their hearts are glad.

Gaping above, as they pray
before their next strategic move,
well planned and well rehearsed.
Marching, squashing them to dust
vanquishing, rejoicing
forever forgetting and wholly forgiving.

An account of such sagas be told
of crazily conflicting and overbearing times.
Revolting against a communist battalion ,
intense bloodshed and hidden crimes.

17. The Ganges River

The Ganga flowing along the ghats.
Serene, pious and full of shine.
A dip in the river
with friends and those who are mine.
A walk along thereafter is absolutely sublime.

Flowing from the Himalayas,
down the mountains
through solid rocks and hilly terrains.
Pure are it's waters
cleansing all sins
as sadhus and pilgrims bathe
together as twins.
Winding it's way through the North of India,
with headwaters like
Alaknanda, Mandakini and Bhilangana.
Flowing down, blessing it's way
filled with flowers and offerings as it sways.

At Varanasi, sitting in a compact, Wooden boat

steering through the ghats as it was afloat.
The night shone bright
with Fire and lights
as the 'Arti' commenced
beyond the fence.
Raising bell's and puja thali's
and chanting captivating hymns
as the engaging public sings.

The heart of Godly love,
the source of all life
the ghats of which every man visits along with his wife.
Children aplenty and friends in toe
a place where ascetics and devotees go.

A Prayer on his lip each passer by hums,
through Haridwar and Allahabad as this river comes.
Watching a holy man,
his forehead besmeared with ashes
has these thick, Brown lashes.
Holding a pot, feeling his matted tresses
perched under a tree, as he caresses
his twisted, long beard
and his sacred thread.

Mystic are the ghats and the river so fine
my eyes as I close in reverence to the divine.

18. Once upon a time

Patterns must dissolve
they happen for reasons unknown.
Accepting them as we do,
or may be sometimes not.

The way I chose to go about
was by recognising my true self,
by praising and worshipping the lord,
by surrendering at his holy feet.

It's your's, I said,
for you to heal.
Me, ever non existent,
that mere dust in his enormous existence.

You must sort, resolve this for me,
for know not I what can be or will be,
neither do I have a solution
nor just any resolution.

Karma they say
I believe it's all just a play.
Just a small figurine
laughing, crying, moving
as you may be keen.

19. Childlike dream

Scintillating dreams, I saw.
Was it London, Mumbai or Paris.
A tale of three cities perhaps
with twinkling lights
and such amazing sights.

A merry go round
Red, Neon, Violet and Blue
and stories that looked oh so true.
It's all happening as if on cue.

The prince and Princess
a fairytale,
man and women
wearing pigtails.
A cart with precious treasures did I see
transported to childhood was this tiny me.
Frocks and fancies
wore the bridesmaids,
walking daintily under those covered, plush shades.

A vivid dream, a happy sequence of
kingdoms and palaces
of so many pretty children and chalices.
A waking dream or visualisation
filled with colours, streams and downright imagination.

Childhood memoirs or childhood romance
call it whatever, am taking this chance
of writing it down
lest I forget
in any jest
these ideas and visions
such dreams and passions.

20. Letting go

Embracing myself
away from barriers and restrictions.
Self imposed may be
perhaps, led by past experiences.

An episode of frivolocity must prevail
nothing serious
but fun and games.
Letting me know it's never too good
to run away from the wants within,
its just so important to bring back that grin.

Self love encompasses all these things
where the heart allows from within
some basic Vodka, Tonic and Gin.
Memories of childhood come flashing by
drinking sips of tangy Gin and Lime,
when each 'Diwali' saw me drink
without any cares or slippery slimes.

Do yourself this favor
enjoy all such tasty, mild flavours.
No boundaries, no actions fake
do until the heart and mind genuinely merry make.

21. Lovers

In love have I found a friend
to cherish and know even more.
No curbs, no shackles
no hurdles any more
for those are days from another yore.
Holding hands as we walk
along the oceans and cosy parks,
sharing stories from spoken lores.

The draft of wind blowing my hair
like a gentle peck on my cheek.
I stride bold and strong
for no longer am I meek.

A gift from God's is this love
straightforward, effortless and undemanding.
How was I so lucky, I ponder
attempting to fly off into the wide spread skies yonder.

Is he for real, my lover so fine

with wavy, bouncy hair
currently munching some roasted cashews
with some fruity, Red Wine.

At times walking towards a temple,
hand in hand
participating in worship and prayers alike
my soulmate, have I finally found him, I think,
thanking the Lord, as I write this in Ink.

With similar tastes and hobbies alike
watching theatre and movies
and arts we like.
His Silvery, White shirt
my heavily embroidered skirt.
His rugged, Denim jacket
and my shirt with its pocket.
We are truly a perfect match.

A night filled with such a dream
is the best one I had
with romance, love and such an intimate theme.